Praise for *What the Deep Water Knows*

"Raw and intimate . . . full of female life—a note scribbled to a son, a hummingbird in the garden, a lover walking away. Surprising and captivating."
— **Jenny Jackson, author of *Pineapple Street***

"How I loved this. Poems that . . . broke my heart and healed it, too. Fans of *The Paper Palace* will adore it."
— **Clare Leslie Hall, author of *Broken Country***

"Raw, honest, and thought-provoking. Brilliant and intentional, you will come back to these pages time and time again."
— **Jessica Urlichs, author of *Beautiful Chaos***

"Breathtaking . . . Heartbreaking, funny, poignant, hopeful . . . this is poetry you didn't know you needed but will change the way you see the world."
— **Daisy Goodwin, author of *The American Heiress***

Praise for *The Paper Palace*

"Tightly woven and immediate, *The Paper Palace* takes us deep into a vivid summer landscape and a longstanding love story, and holds us there from start to finish."
— **Meg Wolitzer, author of *The Interestings***

"A magnificent page-turner."
— **Cynthia D'Aprix Sweeney, author of *The Nest***

"A captivating debut . . . full of lush, atmospheric details."
— ***Publishers Weekly***

"Doubly blessed when it comes to descriptive powers, Heller is as good on nature as she is on interiors."
— ***The New York Times***

"Heller pulls no punches. Some of them just sneak up on you later on."
— *Kirkus*

"It's been ages since I was so absorbe' I loved it."
— **Nick Horn**

What the Deep Water Knows

MIRANDA COWLEY HELLER

Zibby Publishing
New York

What the Deep Water Knows: Poems

Copyright © 2025 by Miranda Cowley Heller

All rights reserved. No part of this book may be used, reproduced, distributed, or transmitted in any form or by any means without the prior written permission of the publisher, except as permitted by U.S. copyright law. Published in the United States by Zibby Publishing, New York.

ZIBBY, Zibby Publishing, colophon, and associated logos are trademarks and/or registered trademarks of Zibby Media LLC.

This book is a work of fiction. Names, characters, places, historical events, and incidents are the product of the author's imagination or are used fictitiously. Any resemblance to actual persons, living or dead, events, or locales is entirely coincidental.

Prepared in association with Penguin Random House UK with acknowledgment of the following permissions: "Salvage," *Sixfold*, summer 2016, pp. 6–8; "Linden Stories," *Sixfold*, summer 2016, p. 9; "More," *Sixfold*, summer 2016, p. 10; "Things the Tide Has Discarded," *Sixfold*, summer 2016, pp. 11–12; "Borrowed Light," *Method Writers Speak, Number Four*, Los Angeles Poets & Writers Collective, 2024, p. 63; "The Difference Between Them," *Ploughshares*, winter 2024–25, pp. 39–40

Library of Congress Control Number: 2025933463
Paperback ISBN: 979-8-9924276-2-2
Hardcover ISBN: 979-8-9924276-1-5
eBook ISBN: 979-8-9924276-3-9

Book Design: Jouve (UK), Milton Keynes
Cover photograph © Blair Resika
Cover Design © Dan Jackson at Penguin Random House UK

www.zibbymedia.com

Printed in the United States of America
10 9 8 7 6 5 4 3 2 1

For my father

At the crest of the hill two stallions,
backs black against a nectar wash,
graze on the green-tang clover,
acorns to sniff out. We lie together
beneath the flowering hawthorn,
your white collar unbuttoned. Once,
I heard the sound of wind under water,
breathed in the sea and survived.

(from *The Paper Palace*)

Contents

ONE

Linden Stories	3
Things the Tide Has Discarded	4
Vertigo	6
Imprints	8
Shadow Puppets	10
The Difference Between Them	13
That Day	15
L'Origine du Monde	17
Sixteen	20
The Yew Tree	22
Circumcision	25
Nestlings	27
Lambing Season, Devon	29

TWO

Milk & Salt	35
On the Day You Were Born	38
Birthday Circle	39
After the Boys Have Left for School	40
Iced Coffee	42
Salvage	43
Amen	47

Red Moonlight	48
Malibu	51
Rehabilitation	53

THREE

Wedding Vows	57
The Way of Tea	59
More	60
Flying Backward	62
Easter, Somerset	64
At the Edge of the Arctic Circle	66
Swallow	68
In the Andes	70
Wait	71
Entrails	73
The Last of the Lilies	76

FOUR

The Taste of Pennies	81
Fox Tale	82
Shooting Crows	83
Gypsy Moths	84
Fear of Falling	86
Blue-Black Depths I Cannot Sound	88
The Weight of Water	89
Cold Storage	91
Lost in Translation	92
Borrowed Light	94

FIVE

Bird Song	99
Fingerprints	100
Plasma	101
Half-Life	102
Try	103
The Earth Is Flat	104
For Dorianne Laux – "Facts About the Moon"	107
Shrink Wrap	108

SIX

Have Faith	115
For Jimmy	117
Wisteria	119
Cambridge Scientists Reverse Aging Process in Rat Brain Stem	120
And What of the Afterlife?	121
The Days Ahead	124
A Peacock's Beauty	126
The Art of Falling	128
The Miracle of Chickens	130
What the Deep Water Knows	131

ONE

Linden Stories

In another world, eggs come home to roost,
chickens hang from the rafters
like fat, auburn-feathered bats,
and my husband is in a good mood every morning.

In another world, my mother sings me to sleep.

In another world, I do not furnish rooms
with no one in them but the dream of a future self.
I sit in my chair every day
and write something good. Or bad.

In another world, a ship sinks, too close to shore.
Villagers row out in their stub wooden boats,
collect a cargo of linden saplings and sacks of millet,
plant a tree whose branches stretch to touch the moon,
making a bridge for us.

Things the Tide Has Discarded

I stand in bare feet at the break,
icy water soaking my cuffs.
A scoop of pelicans dives on bait fish
– relentless, cruel –
kelp fronds mourn them in the glassy deep.
A hermit crab creeping on to shore
skittles its way across the sand.
In the blue, a soot tern wings loop-the-loops.
And I lift my face into the wind.

Farther along the beach, sea lice bite and itch
at damp piles of jetsam – a butter clam rotting in its shell,
a plastic tampon applicator, sea-glassed pink,
crisp hollow straws and green-black weeds.
Things the tide has discarded from its tumbling nest
and then reaches for, stretching its wide arms
in yearning, in regret, before turning away.

I wonder about the sea.
Does she miss the things she leaves behind,
abandons in her wake?

My mother holds the new baby. She offers it
her thick, ripe breast, her puckered nipple,
warm béchamel milk. I watch her soothe and sway,

whisper secrets not meant for me.
At night I wait for her to come,
pull the yellow blanket over my head,
hide from the hollow longing.

A streetlight casts tree-shadows on my ceiling.
Black lace branches dance in the wind.
My room is filled with the breath of ghosts.
I listen to the house – a body turning in a sighing bed,
the long, dark hallway agape.
The silence of floorboards.
Pluck at the glass eye of my rabbit. Rip it off.

Thin threads protrude from a star-shaped hole.
They wave at me, begging for remorse.
I clasp the cold eye in my hand –
a talisman to mute the dread:
the killer waiting in the closet, blazing fire,
my mother dying.
Fear is a pebbled shore of tiny glass eyes.
Think of a white shirt instead.

My mother does not fear death.
All life is ebb and flow.
Earthworms and maggots will feed on her flesh,
a pear tree will grow from her rich soil.
Flowers will bloom on a hillside, she says.
She must not know the picture she paints –
she must not know the things she leaves behind.

Vertigo

Inching my way forward,
dragging my too-big, too-heavy carry-on bag,
I try not to be annoyed
by the woman in the wheelchair holding everyone up.
Ahead of me on the gangway the pilots chat, killing time.
One complains about his vertigo.
That's not what you want to hear
when you're boarding a flight.
You want a captain who understands square roots,
who doesn't lose his balance in the sky.

It reminds me how the tilting sky made me dizzy as a child,
swinging in a hammock strung between white pines,
cradled in thin ropes of hemp. The pit in my stomach.
Reaching with my tiptoes into the warm, wormy soil,
anxious to be rooted to the ground.

I'd close my eyes and picture my father
working in his study, idly picking his nose.
The creak of his leather chair as he leaned back,
chewing on his pencil, hoping for inspiration,
ignoring my mother's insistent voice
calling him to help her with dinner –
the frustration in her tone.

And imagine her, afterward,
when it was only the two of us,
feeding me half an avocado
with olive oil, lemon, and salt.
Letting me stick toothpicks in the slimy pit,
balance it in a jar of water on the window ledge
until white, hoary roots filled the glass,
and a miniature tree magically appeared overnight.

Imprints

My cot is too small.
I put my thumb in my mouth and suck
until the languid pull of dreams lures me
into a restless sleep. Wisps of something sweet.
Slick black forms swimming under clear waters.
Spindle fingers point –
get back from the water. wake up, they want you dead.
Sharp white teeth to scorch your bones
and rip hot flesh.

Tumble back to the dark room,
to the firmly closed door,
back to fear, to the bathroom,
fumbling for the light switch.
The white-tiled room is bright.
The cat curled up under the radiator.
It's a cold night.

I pee, wipe myself properly,
front to back, as I've been taught.
But I'm afraid to flush.
If I wake my mother's boyfriend, he'll yell at me.
Dark, hard, picayune, prickle-hearted child.
I can't take that risk –
when I make him mad she stops loving me.

My chest folds in on itself, squeezing me.
Heart splatters on the floor in clots,
spackles the walls. I kneel on knobby knees,
pick up the pieces of thick-sown blood,
scrub the tile floor clean of traces,
curl beside the radiator and wait for dawn,
for stirring sounds telling me it's safe to flush.
I don't notice the carmine cat-paw prints
scattered across my cheeks,
the telltale smudges of my heart.

There will be a reckoning.

Shadow Puppets

Our second-story apartment overlooked
a parking garage. It stayed lit all night,
made us feel safe when our mother was out.
Every evening, heavy iron bars
lowered across its gaping door.
Three night-guards sat inside,
leaning back in dun-metal folding chairs,
smoking plastic-tipped cigars,
and watched us all in watery relief.
Young girls silhouetted naked in the frosted
bathroom window, steam rising above our shoulders.
Warped, wavering, like women in a Turkish bath.
Saw the outline of a small girl
bent over double to dry her legs.
Of an older sister examining
her soft apricot nipples in the mirror.
Of a heavyhearted mother's sagging breasts,
arms stretched above her head.
Saw our hidden places in shadow puppetry,
exposed by the bare bulb.

Year after year they watched.
I never knew the reason for their knowing catcalls,
their too-familiar contempt as I hurried past them,

face to the gray sidewalk, shoulders hunched forward
in a self-inflicted scoliosis to hide
my budding breasts from their two-fingered whistles.
I made myself into an inverse proportion
until I no longer recognized my own silhouette
in plate-glass windows.

Had I known, I could have crouched
in the dark shadows of my bedroom,
watched them back – playing cards,
radio low, blowing their noses
into blue bandanas, bored, fondling themselves,
anticipating the naked girls in the window,
cursing the rich men in their Mercedes
stinking of cognac and pussy
who buzzed them awake at 4 a.m.

Once, at our summer cabin,
I hid behind the curtains and watched a man
wading in the shallows of the lake,
a threadbare towel wrapped too high around his waist.
His balls dangled out from the bottom.
I stared, repulsed and pulled
by their stretched chicken-skin, their pocked hairiness.
He caught me spying
and dropped his towel into the dappled-drab water.
Smiled at me cock forward, a slow gotcha.
And I ducked in crimson shame.

I wish those men in the parking garage
had exposed themselves to me.
Had I known, I could have crossed the street,
straight-backed. Asked them why
they catcalled my pubescence. My sister's tits.
What are they to you beyond a drink
of warm curdled milk, a suckling memory
of the most tender love you ever had?

Had I known, I could have looked
them in the eyes and said,
My life does not belong to you.
If you steal my image, you steal my soul.
Take your hands off your cocks.
I'm not just a silhouette.

The Difference Between Them

Her sister loved pepper on everything. *Just a little bit more,* she'd say, while the waiter stood there, resentful and impatient, twisting the cumbersome wooden mill over and over again, waiting to be released. For Anna, pepper was a take-it-or-leave-it spice. Anna loved salt. She loved everything about it: its purity, its texture – the way table salt poured out like white sand or could mark the passage of time in an hourglass. That it was iodized. And the rough, harsh crystals of sea salt that still tasted of the ocean. She was even okay with the water retention. She imagined that when the moon was full, the tides inside her body would rise, so swollen and dangerous that she could swallow the shore, obliterate her own wake. Her sister avoided salt: it made her hands blow up like balloon animals, and her wedding ring became a tourniquet cutting off blood flow. Anna had no ring. She hated dependency. And that was another thing about salt: she could shake it out herself, do a test-pour into the palm of her hand to make sure it wasn't pepper, decide how much or how little she needed. There were no politics with salt. She disliked restaurants that didn't put salt on the table: where it was implied, just by forcing you to ask, that you were insulting the chef. She found *that* insulting – the implication that someone else's taste buds were better, that taste could be an absolute.

Her parents had done that – used food as a way to judge them – to criticize or praise. "A" for eating sweetbreads, "F" for refusing the tongue. She'd never understood why she was less worthy than her sister because she didn't like the cow brains their mother served them, intact, in a cast-iron frying pan, like Judith offering them the head of Holofernes for dinner. Once, when her sister was young, she had eaten fish eyeballs. She didn't know she was supposed to leave the head lying on the plate with its sad, blank stare. For years after that, their parents would dig out the tiny, beady eyes with a fork and watch her sister swallow, and she would pretend to like it. The eyeballs had a horrible texture – like tiny, jellied testicles, she told Anna. But they were trained in the art of pleasing. It was so much better than displeasing. Displeasing meant being freezed out – that awful withholding when you had disappointed them. Pleasing – well, that was obvious. When you pleased them, they rewarded you with approval. It had always been a contest: two little girls vying for Best in Show. And how it all shook out is what caused the difference between them: wanting to be infantilized or needing praise, swimming in the deep end or refusing to let go of ancient wounds – who was the favourite, who was loved less, who would inherit the good pearls. Whose breasts he had stroked, who he'd left alone.

It wasn't that she didn't like pepper. Pepper was fine. Punctuation – an exclamation mark, like wasabi. It put the taste right up into your nose – a sudden, raw burn that took you by surprise, even though you'd expected it. It reminded her of the moment just before she cried – when the bridge of her nose flared and stung, numbed by the salt tears she never wanted to shed.

That Day

We were looking for ghosts that day
on the abandoned estate. I said there's no such thing,
and hoped I was wrong.
We leaned our bikes against an old barn
in the suffocating shade. It was so hot.
Even the wind was airless.

Picture frames hung on blunted nails.
A rusted scythe. Sawhorses.
The croquet set we found was missing
so many wickets it was useless.
And the mice carcasses –
musky sweetness of rotting fur.

In an overgrown field, we found a tennis court,
red-clay, screechy, hot cricket grass buzzing world.
The sad remnant of a memory: champagne ghosts
in cream wool pants, buckskin saddle shoes,
pearl cigarette-holder love affairs.
Did they think they were immortal, as we did?

We jumped a dry streambed, rock to rock,
across gray boulders, skins mirrored
with glinting mica in the parched sunlight,
twigs and branches, a beer can caught in their gussets.

Beyond a line of willows, we found the river.
You were afraid there might be water moccasins.

I climbed into the branches of the elder tree,
grabbed the thick-knotted rope,
swung out low over the river – a few test swings –
looking out for snake heads skating
their tick-tack s-curves across the eddies.
A family paddled by in a blue canoe.

The current was strong, but it was so hot that day,
in the stillness of the world.
We swung out together, high and far,
let go at just the right moment.
I remember you, suspended in the air beside me,
as the world held its breath for us.

L'Origine du Monde

How I loathe these drunken artists my stepfather
brings home with him every Friday night,
shouting like bulls about Courbet and de Kooning,
their paint-stained corduroys stinking of turpentine,
hands hennaed in umber and burnt sienna.

Full of self-loathing and vigor, of false comradery.
Full of shit and dreams of perpetuity.
And want pasta to eat, bread to tear
– to sop their ironstone bowls. Wine,
to transform disillusionment into blame.

Roaring, injured krakens.
Cowards, bellowing at the tiny ember.
Who cares about your swathes of color,
your allegories, your academic figures,
your murdered muses?

I hide in the hallway in my frayed flannel nightgown,
watching my mother flirt and smirk, wave her hips
around the dining room as she passes the Bolognese,
pours the red wine, plum-spraying the white linen tablecloth.
Watch the tiny splatters spreading into its tender fibers.

My mother is so beautiful.

She laughs too loud, falls into G's lap,
his blue duck trousers, his oily fisherman's sweater.
He can smell her. I see it in the way
he touches her wrist, in his stiffened prick.
Beside him, L eats a carrot. Noisy, spittled.
An orange speck lands on his sleeve.
A pinch-lipped glance from his silent, white-haired wife.

My mother walks right past him, passes the salad.

My stepfather's beard is a nest of crumbs.
"Stop skulking. Get in here."
I shake my head, no.
"Sing something for us. We need music."
"Yes, yes!" they chorus like snakes.
He waves the salad away.
"Look at this girl. Pure Titian."
They laugh – an uproar.

My mother smiles at me. Venom drips from her nostrils.

Under the din, R leans in with her cigarette-gravel solemnity,
"Come pose some afternoon. I pay six dollars an hour.
I need a young girl who knows how to keep still.
I'm doing harlequins."
"She can't." He rises out of his chair,
tips his glass over, murders the tablecloth,
a dark stain that can never be washed away.

My mother hands me a stack of dirty plates. "Wash these."

She pours back a grappa, spins around.
"We should dance! Samba!"
He grabs her arm. "That's enough."
A sharp bite before turning away
to argue about *L'Origine du Monde*.
White marks appear then disappear on her wrist.

In the living room my mother is dancing
to scratchy bossa nova, green eyes closed.
The swish of her hair against raw silk.
The artists sit and watch her, legs splayed, hoping,
as her dress twirls upward, for a glimpse of quim.

Sixteen

On Tuesdays and Thursdays, he came,
pushing his dinged-up mower through our garden gate,
leather belt of spades and clippers dangling from his jeans.
Black hair, white soil-stained Henley,
skin glazed in sweat and ardor, a dusting of earth.

Once, I saw him staring at my bedroom window
and wondered if he looked for me.
Or was he searching for a wasps' nest to knock
from the eaves; a widow's web, the telltale lines
of gnats trapped between the clapboards.

I dreamed about him coming to my room
some summer day when my parents were out.
How he would unlace his boots, stretch his arms
crosswise above his head, remove his shirt,
and take me roughly on the bed.

This man, who always asked my mother first
before putting down poison for the snails
or pruning her hydrangeas.

One day a robin flew in through my window
when no one else was home. I ran outside,

panicked by its panic, its black-bead eye –
the way it flew at me in angry darts
as if its trapping were my fault.

I followed him upstairs, watched him
corner the anxious bird, cup it in his hands,
careful not to bruise its wings.
Saw the flash of red freedom fly out through the trees.

I stared at the floor while he took off his shirt,
unbuckled his belt. Stared at the robin's thin trail
of fearful urine leading to my windowsill, just before it flew.

The Yew Tree

I travel through my body,
past blood cells, bone, cartilage,
swimming upstream through my heart,
surprised to find no clots, no blockages.
And come, at last, to the Black Hole
in my center. This is why I'm here.
I need to know what gravity
pulls and tugs at my soul.

What dead star inside me
ever burned bright enough
to suck itself into its own mouth?
I need to know.
Do I carry an alternate universe inside me?
Or only stones and concrete blocks
of hardened shames. Clipped nails,
bitten, picked toes, clink of ice in frosted glass.
I worry myself like Greek glass beads.

At the edge of its gravitational pull,
cows and pigs are suspended in midair,
holograms of things that have been sucked
in before me. A man in a pin-striped suit –
my blinkered father – his briefcase

hovering out of his reach.
Palaces and moats of swill-water float past.

My mother standing over the
old enamel stove in the galley kitchen.
She's wearing an apron over her jean skirt,
stirring chicken livers in a cast-iron pan,
frozen in time.
"Go wash your hands,"
she says, "dinner is ready."
"Go wash your hands,"
she says, "dinner is ready."
"Go wash your hands,"
she says, "dinner is ready."

My sister says, "Everyone else can do double Dutch.
Your hair's greasy. Jesus. You smell."
And the man who knocked on the door
at night, whispering, "Are you awake?"

A can clanks against a plate.
I wait for a space in time.
Can't risk getting hit by the body
of a feral cat gnarling, claws out.
Then I jump into the hungry mouth.
My stomach drops with a venal gorgon thud.
In my ears, the whoosh of black blood.

Below me, a pinhole of light opens
like a dog eye in the dark, a lens into myself.
Are you ready for this? Can you take it?
Do you have the guts? I certainly don't.

Feet touch solid ground, sweet birds everywhere.
Flitting clouds of yellow and turquoise wings.
Petal-blessed, free in the wind.
Turnip-pink blush. And a child's voice
singing beyond the rise of a green hedge.
There she is, curled beneath a yew tree,
sucking her thumb.

Her eyes look at me, waiting to be written.
There is nothing behind them,
nothing behind her song. "Here," I say,
and hand her a piece of wheat bread,
a boiled egg, canned cheese. We walk toward
the river, the path between the trees,
leaving our frozen images behind us –
empty holograms stamped on the black night.

Circumcision

Like a butterfly circling its nest,
my mother takes a hair tie
and secures me.
There, darling, she says,
yanking too hard.
Now I can see your face.

If a buttery world existed,
I would like to know it.
But forks and set the table
are the only words I know.
Foreskins are for boys, she says.
You are nothing but a girl.

Pots and pans of rabbit stew bubble.
The bite of onion tears.
I wish for bread.
For milk.
But rabbit it will be, she says,
the shrieking death of lucky feet.

I pounded the pavements of New York.
In rainy London I envied the people
and their dogs – that kind of love.
I felt the earth move under Buckingham Palace,

the guards lilting, fur hats off-plumb,
red coats clattering.

And wondered whether
the ground itself had shifted,
or if I alone had gone akimbo,
bread-starved,
hair flying,
flailing above its crust and soil.

But I will never know anything for sure,
other than where I have walked,
and the mother I was born to follow.

Nestlings

We planted a sweet bay tree in a terra-cotta pot
just outside the kitchen door –
not a *tree* tree, but a delicate thing,
topiaried, like a hothouse kumquat –
and placed it on a paving stone
under a lattice of snap peas.

The tips of their tendrils brushed it
when the wind flared.

One day I found a nest held in its tines,
no bigger than a duck egg,
well hidden among the stiff laurel leaves.
A mouse-brown wren blinked at me.
Her mate hovered, flitting in the branches
of the pear tree on the hill.

Five eggs appeared, tissue-blue,
one speckled brown.

I checked them every day until they hatched.
Saw the first suffocating mass – a pink wound.
Four nestlings survived. Beaks appeared.
A dusting of down. No feathers yet, no song.

Then cheeping. Almost inaudible.
Always hungry for their mother.

The night of the storm the winds blew hard,
bashed the shutters, tipped the nest atilt.

I found it like that: three nestlings
hedged at its twiggy precipice.
A baby bird lay below, stunned,
in the potted earth. I left it there to die.
A mother bird rejects her young
if she smells a human hand.

"Oh, for God's sake," my mother said,
the tight line of her mouth audible through the phone.

"It's a myth. Birds have a terrible sense of smell.
Stick it back in its nest.
Do you honestly believe that mother bird
just spent weeks sitting uncomfortably
on her pile of fragile eggs,
vomiting earwigs into her chicks' mouths,
only to give up the moment some human touches them?"

And I thought, as she hung up, how different my life
would have been if my mother had been a bird.

Lambing Season, Devon

For dinner that night, we grilled fresh sole,
ate duck-fatted potatoes pulled
from the farm's own soil,
backbreaking rows upon rows.
I drank champagne,
blew out my candles.
Eighteen.
A hole-punchable age.
And when the dinner was over
we scraped bones into slop pails,
dried plates with soiled rags,
pulled on our muddy boots,
and headed down to the barn.
Night shift. Lambing season,
when extra hands were hired
on the farm. Lambing season,
where at last my hands
had found a purpose.
I was in love with love that night.
With possibility. With old stone barns,
hard cider and hellebores,
and the sweet smell of manure
on the spring air.
With the farmer's pretty wife,

her hair tied back in a red satin ribbon.
With the farmer's sinewed back.
And the way he had taught me
to mend a broken fence,
careful never to graze the barbed wire.
How he held sharp stalks of grass
between his teeth, leaned back on the hill
as we looked out together at the swelling ewes,
their bums still red with ram's dye,
bellies heavy with child. Looked out
beyond the barns, beyond the restless bulls
stomping in their paddocks.
Looked out to where the brown-black
sinkhole steamed, its brimming mud
a quicksand of corpses
and rotten vegetables.
A place where dead things went
to decay, dissolve into ghosts –
into gaseous fumes that rose in the chill air,
warming it with death.
He told me his favorite mare
had gotten loose and, in her haste
for freedom, leapt into the sinkhole.
He roped her tight, determined,
but the suck and pull
would not let go its prize.
He spoke false comfort in her ear,
watched as her panicked eyes

disappeared by inches
beneath the black-hearted mud.

Night shift, and we headed
down the moonlit road,
down to the old stone barn,
climbed the thousand hay bales
that stepped up from the hard-packed floor
like an ancient amphitheater –
where we could watch over the sheep,
see the sudden writhe of a ewe in labor,
descend the bales.
Stick our ungloved hands
into the warm red muck,
find the tiny legs, the still-soft hooves,
pull hard against the suction
of secret places, lest they suffocate
inside. The unlucky ones
were thrown into the sinkhole,
the warmth of the womb still on them.

Night shift when, on quiet nights
when the ewes were silent,
you could hide between the bales
out of sight, the scratch of hay
raking your back.
Fall in love with a man
who did not belong to you.

Let him make love to you at dawn,
take your virginity
again and again,
speak false comfort into your ear
while the world slept.
And nothing but the scuff
of a bull's horn against a fence post,
the warm huff of sleeping sheep.
Nothing but the baby inside you,
which, you both knew, was destined
for the sinkhole.

TWO

Milk & Salt

I
Milk

My left ovary lived for four short months,
before a surgeon cut it off.
A small, gentle thing full of promises,
tossed into the dung bucket
along with the rest of my tainted flesh.
Later, in my hospital crib, I screamed in soul-hunger,
salted-wound despair. Where was my mother?
Where my mother's milk? Where her warm bosom?
Like a raging elephant chased by lions across the dry savanna,
she abandons her sickly young.

Tiny fists punched the air, tore open stitches.
They tied my hand to the bars of the crib.
"Such a good baby," said the nurse,
adjusting the binding around my wrist,
pulling it tighter and tighter.

Bright lights that never dimmed glared into my eyes,
into my cot, its white sheets speckled
with the drops of red blood that slurried down my side.
A pigeon hit the plate-glass window,
leaving a trail of white gunge as it slid.

My loose hand gripped a rattle in its fist,
shaking it like a lifeline.
"Now the other hand," she said.

II
Salt

"Babies cry," my mother said, boasting of her parenting.
"If you ignore them long enough, eventually they'll stop."
And left us all to cry into the corners of our cribs,
sweaty, hair-scrunched tangles of fear, frustration, sorrow.
Until the night my guts burst, leaking deep
into my shadow-places. I screamed for her in pain
but still she did not come.

How was he? I ask my mother when we
get home from the movie –
"Perfect. He cried himself to sleep
and now he's sleeping like a baby" –
and want to hit her, red-slap-handprint her,
except I can't decide
whether it's her face I should slap or mine.

And could I stop this fist in fork
hot pepper reef shark rage – the battery-acid tears I hold,
refusing to relinquish? As if to steep
in an infant's rage is an action of defiance.
So careful not to spill the endless bitter.

Keep two hands around the silver cup,
a balanced book atop my head,
walk straight-backed, crimped, soft-slippered.

I wonder, if I spilled them now,
poured every drop into the flowerpot,
would flowers bloom?

I watch him sleeping in his crib,
the rise and fall,
the mingled smell of milk and salt,
and promise him a better life.

On the Day You Were Born

I longed for language:
create a fish with my fist,
ludicrous, clairvoyant,
peaches, polyglot foraging,
plankton, funnel,
tainted price of a hair's breadth.
What are words for "clear"?
Window?
Water?
Glass?
Something unwittingly beautiful –
so unwittingly beautiful
that we cannot even see it.

Do you know what infinity feels like?
It feels like this.

Birthday Circle

The Lord was at his son's birthday circle.
Sugar-free popsicles had been passed out.
A song had been sung. Now, one by one,
the teacher asked the children to praise their classmate.
"He's fast in Gym," the first boy said.
"He's funny," a girl giggled.
"He runs fast," a third child said.
The fourth raised his hand. "I have a question."
"Okay," the Lord said, "but you only get one, so make it a good one."
"If hippos are so dangerous, why did you make them look cute?"
"Good question," the Lord replied.
"Is that why girls have vaginas?" the little boy asked.`
"I said one question," the Lord replied.

After the Boys Have Left for School

I stand at the kitchen sink. Stare into the back garden.
Vague. Flat sky. Rubber gloves. Ponder:
Why do we hate squirrels less than rats?
Do the clouds float by us, or are we turning with the earth?
Is it sky that fills the universe – is it as simple as night?
What's in the locked blue box on my son's desk?
Do dishwashers really save water?

Water drip-drips from the tap, filling nothing.
It needs to be fixed. California's in a drought.
And, really, the pool should be emptied.
But I always think that when the Big One comes,
flinging rats and squirrels from the trees,
shattering French doors and flatscreens,
bending bridges, crushing us in our cars,
swallowing us into fissures,
and palm nuts rain onto cracked sidewalks,
if we survive, the water in the pool will come in useful.

We can drink and bathe. Boil water for tea.
Eat ramen. I have purifying tabs, a LifeStraw,
waterproof matches, astronaut food, powdered milk,
tampons, a hand-crank radio, a silver whistle,
Mylar blankets in tiny packets that are meant to do
something in a crisis . . . a machete I cannot wield.

And a pencil and paper to leave a message for my boys:
I went to your school to find you.
If I miss you there, wait for me at home.

Or, as they texted when the plane went down,
I will love you forever.

But what if the pool cracks and all the water
disappears into the ground? What then?
Tighten the faucet.
Dry your hands on your jeans.
Look away from the window.

Iced Coffee

The boy sits next to his mother.
Pimples pronounced, wide-bridged nose,
teen-drab hair. Scorn. One day he'll be handsome.
He drinks cold coffee. It's easier to swallow.
No waiting for it to cool.
No timing it just right between
the first small sip, the blowing,
and the next attempt.
Those are things we learn in time –
how not to scald your tongue.

She picks up her phone.
Talks to someone else. He listens, takes a sip.
waiting for her to do the same for him.
She shifts in her chair, jangles her wrist,
wags her high-heeled boot.
The table rocks. It needs a matchbook.
She wants to look young for her age.

He bites off a hangnail, whittles it in his teeth,
wonders who will inherit her big gold ring.
That bangle. It's not that he wants her to die. Ever.
He's just thinking ahead to when his skin clears,
his shoulders broaden. When the person he loves sees him.
When he can drink hot coffee without getting burned.
When he knows how to calibrate temperature.

Salvage

After our basement flooded
I waded through cardboard boxes,
their sodden, drooping bottoms
coming apart in my hands,
and wished I had put them on cinder blocks.
Boxes of memories, electric cords,
hairpins, curves. Cassettes, tangled and unwound:
wisp-thin seaweeds of magnetic tape
filled with lost songs.
Baby clothes, rust-soaked and rotting,
each tiny sock, shirt, desiccated elastic waistband,
a familiar note. And endless tax receipts
in case they came asking for proof of the past.
I threw out a Sega, a shredder,
three Styrofoam gravestones stamped
Rest in Pieces.
A king-sized mattress, plush and coil,
that had sponged up the first of the flood.
It took four of us to drag its
bloated corpse to the street.
Silverfish scattered into city drains.

In the afternoon, I unzipped
a black-and-green tartan suitcase I'd salvaged
– wedged between an etching of *Columbus in Chains*

and a rabbit-eared TV.
Somewhere, there's a photograph
of my mother boarding a train,
her graceful ankles bare, in steep stilettos.
She's smiling at someone.
A porter stands behind her,
holding the plaid suitcase,
a round hatbox under his arm.

Inside the case were all the photos
I thought I'd lost when we moved, years ago.
Many were ruined – water-blurred and tacky,
stuck together in chunky mille-feuilles rectangles,
faces and moments washed away,
bleeded together forever –
left to rot under the floorboards,
the damp, flooding, rat-shit,
sad, dark unearthednesses.

I laid out my past on the kitchen counter,
sifted through the ingredients of my life:
the exact minute my first son was born,
squalling in a doctor's arms,
his umbilical nub dressed like a wound.
Then, he's in my arms in a hospital bed,
latching on to my breast, suckling, pig-perfect.
A phone line runs across me, uncoiled,
stretching as far as it can.

I was talking to my mother –
telling her I'd just given birth to a son.

And the day I fell in love with my husband.
He is standing next to a white Vespa
in a chambray shirt, hair still damp
from a plunge into the Sargasso Sea.
In the photo he took of *me*, I'm naked,
full-frontal, Polykleitan, goddess thighs. Lush.
Wading knee-deep in Bloody Bay.
Afterward, we had sex in the turquoise water
and he didn't tell me when he saw the shark.

Around dinnertime, I picked up the phone
and called my eldest son. He likes to tell me
he's always been unhappy.
But I remember him running across flaxen fields,
wind-lapped, diving into the tumbling stream,
swimming in the deep end.
Eyes bright. Loving me back.
I wanted to tell him I'd found a decade
of proof that he was wrong, that I was right.
In photo after photo he's laughing,
splashing through light.

His phone rang a few times
before going to voicemail, and I felt
the emptiness of boxed air.

But I knew what he would have said
if I'd reached him:
"How do you know I'm not crying
in all the photos that got destroyed?"
And I'd have said:
Because I remember. I remember everything.
And you have to believe me when I tell you
it's worth it in the end, so please stay the course.
A thousand moments, some lost, some found,
and joy and pain and bliss.
It passes through your fingers. And you ask:
How can so much have happened?
How can nothing have happened?
And still, it's everything.

Amen

"There must be some mistake," the Lord said.

Red Moonlight

If I could climb to the top of the highest tree,
what would I see besides fields of shit
and bodies of gutted pigs floating belly-up in brine?
Would I see a bright light far away?
Would it pierce the demon skies with acute beauty?
Would I swallow what I could just in case
the light might stay with me?

I hope so, because I think I'm going to try it.

My son once wrote, *I love the way trees*
grow up and down at the same time.
In his story he dug his roots into the soil,
journeyed through the chthonic undergrowth,
the molten core of the earth, and came out the other side.
I don't remember where. I only remember
the concrete sidewalks that blocked his way
when he tried to burst forth from the earth unharmed.

Oh, how I love that child. And how I hate him for it –
for a heartbreaking love that's more than my body can hold.
He wounds me, panics my soul with turkey briar and wood cockle
and vehemence. I can't stand it, I yell. You're eighteen years old!
Stop asking, "Where are my shoes?" in that plaintive,
worried voice. Put your fucking shoes by the front door at night.

It pains me to think of you out in the world alone.
Learn to do laundry. Separate colors.
Buy toilet paper before it runs out.

He hangs his head in shame and walks away,
shoulders hunched against the bitter winds
of dark city streets, buildings that push into him
like angles of cold light.
I feel the sickening lurch of eels in my heart,
because I love him so. And I grieve for him.
My body is a pierced-through jangling mass
of the fears I carry. Imagine a stomach cavity
filled to the brim with sharp pieces of bitten fingernails.
A lifetime's worth of worry that never got digested.
When they cut me open, they'll say,
Strange calcium deposits here. Sharp and brittle.
We think she died of fear.

I wish I could promise him crisp white linen,
the scent of orange blossoms and mint,
on an early sky. But that would be a lie.
Instead, I say: Never bare your soul.
No girl is interested in a needy man,
no one wants to suffocate in love, not even me.
This is the advice I give my tall, rangy child
who only wants to love and be loved, trust that
the love he gives will not be scorned.
Protect yourself, I say – from ravens that caw,
crawl up your spine, and insects you can't escape.

You want to stop the buzzing in your ears,
but you can't. I can't. Dirt will fill your mouth and nose.
This is the way it is.
Whatever you do, the outcome is the same.

It's the journey that's different.
The journey can be made in shadow or in sunlight.
That's the only choice you get to make.
But if you are in the desert, you'd better travel at night.
The moon will light your path. A red moon
that strokes your back softly and says, I love you.
All will be well, I love you.

Malibu

I took a walk with a mom from school this morning.
She arrived at 8:15.
"After drop-off," she said. The air was still cold.
I don't know why she wanted to walk with me –

I barely know her.
She followed me down the wooden steps to the beach,
picked her way carefully around the rocks.
The sea was a streak of blue.

A humpback whale swam past.
I could hear the blowholes – that's how close, in the kelp.
A sea-lion carcass tumbled in its wake,
bobbed along behind the whale, before sinking into the deep.

In the shade of an overhang,
huddled against the stilts of my neighbor's house,
a seal pup waited, resigned, to be taken by the tide.
I read it's the radiation from Japan that's killing them.

She told me she'd miscarried twice,
she's clinically depressed,
takes sleeping pills at night. Temazepam, 15 mg.
Sometimes half an Ambien.

Dolphins swam the length of the beach, slowed to pace us.
The herring must have been running.
She kept exclaiming every time she saw a fin,
which was every five seconds.

We took off our shoes and stood together,
letting the tide pull at our cuffs.
I told her my son had overdosed at Christmas,
and that that makes me want to die.

Rehabilitation

Afterward (and in those first unholy hours),
I thought about him dying, forcing myself to swallow
the bitter dew of relief, imagining again and again
the "what if" he hadn't woken –

the void hollowing my world forever.
My back-hobbled bare-knuckling-it,
scrunched in pain, cripple fingers knotty.
Because I can still see *him*, but he can't see me.

It cannot happen. I *will* it not to happen.
I only ever want to know my beautiful boy alive
in my own lifetime. I want to see him grow branches,
leaves, lime-green conkers, briar-skinned but rich inside.

I want us to jump over cow pies and tickle grass
until we reach the shade of the dogwood with our picnic lunch,
spread our checkered cloth on the ground
to protect us from ants and damp.

I want him to leap into the sky.
Feel the rush of fresh air and the falling
in his stomach until the water catches him,
carries him downstream to a safer bank.

He climbs out dripping, for once stops thinking
about what has happened,
or what might happen,
or what never will. No more panic.

And lies on the mossy bank.
Sees that he has a body, a fresh pink skin
in the here and now. Legs, arms, a penis, ten toes,
and a spring to cleanse him.

THREE

Wedding Vows

1.

My stomach is full of streaming green lilies,
of seeping tides and prickly-delicious sea urchins
and the hopes and dreams I could never admit out loud.
I drink in the honey of us until I can fill no other spaces
inside me – until even my fingertips smell sweet.

I was never so happy as when we lay,
entwined, beneath the lace-leafy branches
of the river birch, watching soldier ants
carrying their tiny loads up and down the rutted bark.
You touched my hair, and I felt, for once, unburdened.

2.

Here in our new dream house,
many hands make polished glass,
furniture creamed in beeswax.
Brass gleams. The trees are pollarded, privet hedged.
You keep your port in a temperate cellar.

"I promise you the world," you said,
when we took our vows.

And yet I lie awake at night
beside your shiftings under eiderdown,
hearing the rasp of your snores.
I cannot find sleep in this big house.

"I want to give you the world," you said.
Give me something priceless instead:
a good night's sleep.
Sleep cannot be purchased.
Sleep has a mind of its own.
Sleep does what it wants.
Sleep can wear a hat at the dinner table,
put its elbows on the table,
use the wrong soup spoon,
talk back to your mother.

Midnight, and the moon's a bucket of silver beans,
a silent rattle at our window,
shadow-casting you in thread-count sheets.
Give me a lumpy mattress
filled with all the drainings of our love.
Give me the familiar sounds of taxicabs,
street-cleaning at dawn,
the swoosh of city streets, a distant horn.
Fuck you. *Move*, asshole.

Give me back our old life.

The Way of Tea

The flowers strewn across the tatami mat look real.
I reach out to touch one, but the museum guard
steps forward, clears his throat. I move back a few inches.
He hovers until I relent a bit further.
A small placard says the flowers symbolize
the breaking of boundaries, beauty refusing to be contained.
The people in this country love to make rules they cannot break.
I wish I could steal one, take it home.
A perfect peony carved in wood, detailed and delicate.
Beauty that will last forever,
scattered here on the floor just to make a point.

I think about the time I came home
and you had left a trail of rose petals
all the way to the bathtub, scented candles lit.
It was our anniversary.
How, instead of joy, my first thought had been:
After all these years together,
how can he not know I hate scented candles?
I soaked in bubbles, drank the champagne, had sex in the tub,
never letting on that the whole romantic gesture
had made me disappointed in our marriage.
That it would come to mark the anniversary
of the beginning of the end.

More

Hours later, I can still smell his sweet-sour sweat,
his traces, sleep-wrinkled into the pillow;
feel the watered grit, gruel-thin trail, drying on my thigh.
And picture how wordlessly he crept around our room,
stabbing for things in the semi-dark,
trying not to wake me.
I could hear the town car lurking, impatient,
outside our house in the quiet gloam –
that cusp of night and day beyond the windowpane.
A few stars struggled to stay alive in the hushed eggplant sky.
He kissed my forehead, muttered goodbye.

I listened to his footfalls,
his roller bag strumming our cindery walk,
rattle-plastic ball bearings on cement.
Watched him from the window.
He stopped, mid-step, his back to me, picked up his bag,
so careful not to disturb the neighbors
whispering dreamed things in their lingering REM.
Lifted it three inches off the ground,
extended handle wedged in his armpit,
awkward, shoulder shrugged to ear.
And I thought of the way he would
swing our son when he was little,

always begging for more –
more height, more levity.

I watched as the black car
rounded the corner, away from me.
Watched as the streetlights dimmed,
one by one, in the gray quiet.

Flying Backward

At five in the morning when the winds
came up, and the rains had finally stopped,
it was the window rattling against its bearings
that woke me. Pine trees bent sideways, howling.

The pool umbrella lifted from its mooring,
rose a few feet before crashing into the rosebushes.
And the birds – swarming helpless in the relentless
circular current, like fall leaves wheeling through the air.

I nudged you awake. I wanted you to see the maelstrom.
It seemed worth it. Wrens and finches, skylarks
tumbling through the dawn sky – airborne, but not in flight.
You groaned and turned your freckled back to me.

In the corner of the garden, away from the fray,
three ruby-throated hummingbirds thrummed,
holding their ground in the air. Their iridescent wings
beat invisibly fast. A flash of gemstones in the gray sky.

Flying backward. Not pushed, but deliberate,
pressing for a thicket of branches,
the white-blooming hydrangea.
Their wings, attached with tiny wrists,
made figure eights, infinity symbols.

62

I remember reading somewhere that hummingbirds
can fly backward and forward at equal speed:
thirty miles an hour.
I watched them now, frantic with purpose.

If I could fly backward, I would.
To the safety of branches, to the time
when my heart still raced for you,
twelve hundred beats a minute.

Easter, Somerset

The combe rises steep and close
beyond the windowpane. A fifty-foot swell
of comfrey, spring grass, and turf.
A tidal wave of green. A choking gloam.

I stare into the dusk, the leaden rains,
the dark entombing sward; stone steps
hoary with moss, leading nowhere.
A lone cow silhouetted against the sky.

At the flat line of the hill, wooden posts
and barbed wire follow the curve of the crest –
a horizon line of witch's teeth, a dead king's crown,
keeping the cows from the combe.

We are drowning in a rising tide.
Water funnels from all sides, puddles against the kitchen door,
Tulips founder. Hellebores weep. The clock ticks.
My husband chops celery in silence.

The dog runs in and shakes his coat,
settles on the hearth in the warm flicker where our boys
are roasting sausages. They throw fat scraps to him,
delighted each time he catches the meat in flight.

A dung beetle climbs the wall, feeling its way forward.
My husband crushes it under the heel of his hand.
Says, "We need carrots."
I reach for my raincoat, but he lurches out into the dim.

A daub-pink house slowly sinking in the land,
as darkness plunges from the lowering sky
above the barbed-wire crown of thorns,
the cows pressing the fence for give.

At the Edge of the Arctic Circle

I open my fingers and let the rope slip from my hands.
Watch, as the ice floe dwindles,
your figure crouched low on its back.
In that final moment, you said nothing.

It's my fault, in the end.
I untied the bowline,
made us into a slipknot instead.
Settled for good, then mediocre,
then leaving the house for the gym
without bothering to sing out,
"I'm going to the gym!"

For a while, we could still tread water,
circling each other, barely tethered.
Two separate lives, entwined, but unraveling,
the rope that frays, salt water, rot.
Until it gave way to free fall. No net.
Only a sea of tears that could not break our fall.

Standing on the brink of the world,
I watch you disappearing.
Above me on the edge of the cliff
emperor penguins prepare to jump.
I imagine their joy, their forward momentum

as they swim out together, one body, into deeper waters.
I imagine the ice melting beneath you, its hollow crack,
your lonely sink into the depths, my solitary life.
And ask you for forgiveness.

Swallow

I was in love. I was lusty. I galloped across a field of corn,
its grass-green stalks embracing, hiding me inside their secret.
That was the way of bees and sex, love among the ruins,
a fine fuck on a fine day in a fine field of corn.

And then the bleak reality of a cat's paw, the bland wane light,
hoofbeats on dry earth, fallow, what once was verdant.

I meant to plead with you.

"I think you're perfect," you said on our first date. 1989.
"Don't," I said. "I can be a total bitch." And you laughed,
delighted by my honesty. But that day's long gone.
There's too little "me" left to blurt.

Now we eat breakfast apart. Strong espresso, warm milk.
"Try not to scald it." Can't bend down to kiss me –
his back hurts. But he bends to feed the dog,
drinks his coffee on the stoop.

I can't bear this, and I can. And that's the conundrum:
the ability to bear it, to carry a load of shit
even when your limbs have already given way.

Under the table, I watch my thighs jiggle like fat rising to the top
of turtle soup in Kyoto, mallow lard, whale blubber.
Did you know sperm whales ejaculate four hundred gallons of
sperm at a time? That's one thing I don't need to swallow.

This morning when I asked him what time he'd be back,
he gave me that stare and said, "Why?"
I looked at him, ventriloquizing my rage.

I did not say, "Your son's concert is tonight."
I did not say, "I'm roasting a chicken."

In the Andes

Every so often, when I'm eating too fast or chewing gum,
I bite the inside of my cheek and in that quick, surprised pain
am reminded of how chewy flesh is, how warm and rubbery.
How thinly we are layered over.

I think of those rugby players who crashed in the Andes.
The snow, their thin coats, their endless shivering, their terror.
How, when they ate their dead teammates, they complained
that some body parts were too tough, not worth the eating
(unless, as then, in desperation), while others melted in your mouth.

I wonder whether the inner walls of my mouth
would have the delicate, luxurious taste of braised pork cheeks.
And whether pigs bite their tongues or inner cheeks in fear
as they are walking to the slaughter.

Wait

I know I'm fucked the second he says, "Salmon."
It'll be disappointing, and he'll be chippy.
That's the thing about ordering grilled salmon
in a coffee shop. But I don't say anything,
because that would be me being bossy and controlling.
I stare at the slats of the café chairs –
the way the heavy sunlight lances their backs,
black dirt ingrained in swirls of wood, shellac wearing off,
slowly chipping away like a thin coating of brickle.

He says we need a marriage counselor.
Too many resentments have built up.
He wishes he hadn't tried to cover his feelings all these years.
I stare at the cast-iron legs of the chairs and try to figure out
how, exactly, their folding mechanism works –
how they stack together so neatly
when they're put away at night.

He says his shrink has made him realize
maybe all his rage and self-pity are unjustified.
I say, "Yeah," and let the tears drip
from under my dark glasses.
When our waitress leaves the check,
I smile and hope she can't see me.

A splotch of apricot jam has fallen off my bread
onto the side of the table. I watch it sliding down
at the pace of glass. I want to wipe it away
before it lands on my thigh, but I know he'll be annoyed
if I try to clean it while he's talking.
He takes two twenties out of his wallet, and I say, "Wait."
Because I know that once the money is there we'll stop talking.
And I know that, if we stop, it will be the end.

On the table a single pat of salted butter melts in the heat,
a warm, oily trickle on cheap white porcelain – tiger ghee.
I'm angry at myself for eating the bread and butter,
but heartbreak makes me eat.
I bat my dangly arm and watch the way it slows to a stop.
"Wait," I say. "Wait."

Entrails

It's the time I slept in the car
that still sticks me in the guts.

My threats
I can't stay here with you another second.
You're an emotional terrorist.

Then leave.

Expecting you to come out of the house, drag me back in,
parallel-parked on the dark city street. Any minute now.
I was so happy when I heard the dogs bark,
saw the front door pull open, saw you coming.
You put the trash in the bin, went back inside, locked the door.

The nothingness. I felt it.
A streetlight threw its sheer acid halo,
exposing me in the driver's seat.
I cowered, a hundred feet from our front door.

Two men walked past looking for a car to jack –
no one walks in LA at night. I waited until their steps
retreated before pulling into the driveway, headlights off.
I hoped you wouldn't hear the engine.
I wanted to seem resolute.

4 a.m.

Defeated.
Broke into the house.
Stole a toothbrush
and clean underpants.

Our house filled with bowls and books and thirty years.
Children's shoes, art and age. The ghosts of three dogs,
Plaster-of-Paris paw prints. And the cat, no paw to print –
eaten by a coyote, disemboweled, his entrails
left on the street in front of our house like a taunt.
You shoveled his scattered carcass off the pavement.
I heard you vomiting behind the laurel hedge.

5 a.m.

Drove to Beverly Glen and sat in a Coffee Bean,
waiting for our 7 a.m. with the marriage counselor.
I was sure I'd look pathetic, stand out –
who the hell's in a Coffee Bean at that hour?
But the place was already chock-full of women in Lululemon.

7 a.m.

You walked right past me, grim-faced,
taking in the Breuer chairs, the seventysomething

therapist, round glasses that magnified her eyes,
like one of James's wicked aunts before the peach
begins to roll downhill.

Boxes of pre-Vasolined tissues strategically placed
for my tears. Already the hunched shell of an ex-wife.
Limp, powerless, stale coffee breath.
Only my underpants fresh.
I let out a ghastly sob.

We keep missing by inches.

You looked at me with such cold eyes.

Stop being manipulative.
I'm not planning to eat your entrails,
I just want to cut out your heart,
leave you flattened in the road.

The Last of the Lilies

The sun rises, sets over the winter sky,
the snow baring patches of ground.
In the spring, I cooked you ramps
for dinner and you hated them –
threw apples and rotten fruit.

I knew, then, everything
I had always known:
that you loved and hated me both.
That forever is only a flash in the pan.
That love is transient, phonetic.

I can sound the word on the tip
of my tongue. Taste shorthand on my lips.
Remember you in the taste of your cigarette breath,
of unfiltered yogurt, Gentleman's Relish.
Hear you in the pulse of my fatigue.

Do I seem angry? Because I'm not, I'm sad – is what you said.
And I said: *Um, yeah . . . you seem hateful
and filled with virulent rage.*
You put your fist through the wall.
Threw a chair. Set the house on fire.

I watched it all go up in smoke.
Sat outside on the dampened grass,
staring past the last of the lilies, the dog shit
that hadn't made it into the doggy bag,
as your anger smothered us all.

FOUR

The Taste of Pennies

In our last year it flickered, still beating
in the spaces between the distance and the quiet,
your cold hollows, mysterious and grave.

The knowledge of the women came after the end,
though the women came before.
Seething, scarlet, red-silk liars.

Alone at the kitchen table, I still
listen for the click of your key,
the gust of an opening door.

I long for the sound of wind.
Any kind of wind.
A howl a whisper a prayer.

Somewhere upstairs there's laughter.
Our children playing video games,
oblivious.

Only the machine-gun rat-a-tat,
the happy drone of childhood, to keep me sound.
The end of a marriage tastes like pennies.

Fox Tale

A red scarf floats down the cobbled London street.
In the midnight shadows a fox stops,
listens to my footfall, considers running.
But, feeling safe, goes back to the small brown garbage pail,
to the scraps and cuttings and cucumber peels,
the coffee grounds, a chicken bone – a thumbtack.

That was never the plan.
He will take it back to his den
inside his fox belly.
Punctured by the smallest thing
that glinted
and could not be resisted.

Shooting Crows

A flash of silver,
cool mercury streak in his eye.
The half sweet smile, quickening furrow.
His lies have a tell.

If a bird flew from his mouth,
if I caught it, held open my palm,
said, *Here is a white, feathered thing,*
he'd deny it.

So, I catch the bird,
hide it behind my back, smile, let it go.
Collar, scent, receipt – the endless banal.
I hear it flutter, rise up,
a beating thing, the silence of my white lie.

He likes shooting at crows –
the spray of black tail-feathers against blue.
The outraged cackle.
Sometimes I watch him from the porch,
remembering that we, too, once knew flight.

Gypsy Moths

Thick swarmings of gypsy caterpillars cover every tree trunk,
branch – tupelo, oak, pine, beech.
Three hairy backs, three sets of feet,
prickly, thick, snake toward their prey.

These woods I know so well are filled with unfamiliar sounds –
a dim chorus of laser-sharp beaks chomping leaf by leaf.
The soft patter of leaf-shit peppers the sandy ground
like a summer rain.

They've moved in like locusts. Set up tents in our backyards,
nurseries of death. Each sticky cocoon throbs with
the plague it holds. Tough, larval.
I kill what I can reach.

I hear a death knell in the wordlessness of the woods,
its stoic impotence. These trees
that can only stand, stock-still,
while their enemies eat them alive.

As if on cue, a new sandstorm of moths appears,
fluttering around my car.
Brown paper wings beat at the tinted glass.
My windshield wipers splice them in a sudden burst of
murderous joy.

Males. The females cannot fly. They wait for their lovers
on rough-barked trunks, pretending indifference.
But the slight, anxious twitch of their pallid wings
betrays them. Their clocks are ticking.

They only have one week to mate – to seed death, steal the
lapping green.

Fear of Falling

Before we fell, your words were like poppies,
a field of lipstick kisses, red-zip clever,
lusty tulip-crazed promises.

I fiddle my rings.
Count the king palms, their lower bark
painted white in self-protection.

The flowers in their shade smell
of mango, beautiful danger.
Their berries are deadly.

Another look at my phone.
The vacant-lot echo. A cold swim
in the hotel pool would be refreshing.

Neediness puddle-sticks me.
I should order a pressed lemonade.
A lemon sun. Make an offering.

Above me, like a fleeting thought winging its way
across the chipped blue sky,
tiny birds write V for victory.

Can you imagine having wings?
Can you imagine escaping the shark's jaws,
the lion's jaws, the height of the trees?

Effortless in the wind shear. Bat, eagle, blue jay.
Can you imagine? No fear of falling,
no fear your plane will drop from the sky?

Forget the useless life jackets
under or between the seats.
Give us each a tiny parachute.

We could sail softly down to the open sea.
Bob there on the surface
like stunned jellyfish.

Blue-Black Depths I Cannot Sound

"I do still love you," you said last week.
And the room began to spin for me, a twirling belief
that you might realize your misguided stupidity,
that the flecks of rubble-dust, the streaming rain,
the opaqueness of long-lingering grief would suddenly lift.
A swell rose in my heart from my deep ocean drown,
and I said, "So there's hope?"

You were all remorse as you shook your head, no.

The Weight of Water

It's the hole in the screen
that worries me.
One night, a bird flew in.
I hid beneath the covers,
knowing a braver person
would get it out with a broom.

A breeze riffles the oak,
sun-ponding the grass beyond it.
The old blue door is pleasing.
I'm glad I don't have a cat,
sad that the rich peonies are
already dropping their petals.

I wish I were brave enough
to tell you the whole truth.
It's all there in a laptop folder,
pulsing in WordPerfect:
my lies to you, my truths.
Not even the weight of paper.
Not even the weight of water,
or a fir tree, or a blue whale.
Heavier than that. And weightless.

Yellow wildflowers have
covered the hillside like mustard seed
in the killing fields of France.
If you could read my mind,
it would tell you such terrible stories,
you would finally be able to forgive yourself
for leaving me behind to bleed out.
So, I keep my secrets.

Tonight, I will sleep inside.
I will shut the door behind me.
I will bring a broom.

Cold Storage

In the throat of the jade-green vase
the mallows have finally opened.
I have always loved that vase, its elegance,
its ancientness, its great-great-grandmother-ness.
It sits on a dusty shelf through empty autumns,
dark winters, late springs, patiently awaiting summer
when again it will be full of flowers.

I eat a few chunks of pineapple from a plastic container.
Sweet-delicious, good for bruises.
My legs, my thighs, my ankles, biceps
are covered in bruises, some fading, some fresh.
I've been moving furniture all week,
trying to get the scent of my ex-husband
out of his old study – make it my own.
But every time I bang into anything,
even the slightest breath of a touch,
I come up in bruises. A hemophiliac in hiding
under the skin. My internal bleeding
always partially hidden, blue and obscure.

Last summer I packed up his things.
Clothes from the closet, artworks, books.
Put everything in a storage unit for "if and when"
he wants to collect his thirty years of life
with me, I told him. So far, he hasn't come.

Lost in Translation

My dog sniffs around my ankles on the porch,
leans in toward my avocado toast,
disguising desire as vague interest.
But he catches me watching him
and lies on the jute rug, resigned,
all black and white and rust.
When I reach for a bite of my sandwich,
my dog looks at me with the soul of the earth in his eyes,
a look of such longing and love. It might be for me,
or it might be for the sandwich.

If I could speak his language, I would say:
Listen, you won't even like it. It's vegan.
If I could speak his language, I would say:
I doubt tomatoes are good for you
anyway. Or maybe that's just grapes.
If I could speak his language, I would say:
I love you so much, but your breath stinks
and when you lick me with kisses you leave
the faint scent of rotten fish on my arms.

If I could speak his language, I would tell him:
You have saved me these past two years,
given me comfort, devotion, someone to talk to
as I make myself dinner, sleep beside me,

bark at strangers, chase away the fox
that likes to shit on the picnic table,
proclaiming it as his domain. And by the way,
if you speak fox, can you tell him to stop?

If I could speak your language, I say to him now,
I would tell you I lost the man I loved because,
as it turned out, we didn't speak the same language, either.
So, it's not just you. But still, please don't leave me.

Borrowed Light

The sky opens with an outbreath,
revealing her golden egg-yolk belly.
Dawn rises over the sea
with the jingle of sweet glass.
I hike my skirt above my knees
and wade into the shallows,
feel the lunar pull of tides against my shins.

A breeze kicks up, pushing foaming white crests
that come for me, one after the next,
after the next, after the next.
Disquiet tinges the shimmering pink.
My salty lips and cheek. Fingers wind-chapped.
The memory of a peach, a ring,
a chair thrown at a wall.

I cup my hands, gargle but do not swallow
the taste of the sea – each fish/scale/weed and coral/
shipwreck, corpse/mermaid's purse/
the moonlit swims we took.
You were wearing shorts the day you left,
which always felt banal.
Did you mean to be demeaning?

Beyond the circling gulls, beyond their ugly shrieks,
the moon invades the day –
a pale discus tossed up by the horizon,
trying to sneak past the sun, rise unnoticed,
preferring to stun us later.
It's a showman's trick, you know.
A magician's handkerchief.

If you go backstage, you'll see that the moon
is nothing more than a pitted rock
basking in the honey-blaze of the sun,
trying to steal the show.
That what held me in your orbit
all those years was only a mirage.
That what I mistook for beauty
was only borrowed light.

FIVE

Bird Song

Every spring, the stubborn finch
makes her nest in the bower of roses
directly over the French doors
leading out to the vine-covered pergola,
the long table – the doors we use all spring, all summer.
And every year, every time we open the doors,
slamming open, slamming shut,
every time I walk outside with a handful
of knives and forks, napkins, plates,
she panics, flies about startled, wings stuttering,
crashing the glass windows as if it's the first time.

It's just so shortsighted.
Perhaps a finch is like a goldfish –
no long-term memory.
But then how does she know to come back
to the same wrong place year after year?
My shrink asks me the same question.

Fingerprints

I cannot say why I still long for you.
Forever, for forever.
I've measured time in ounces,
the tangent of a star corner,
and still, I cannot say.

You worried me like a bead, sand-stormed me.

Once, I had a fingerprint all my own.
Now, rubbed off, chewed, bitten, nubbed.
I am a ghost on an inkpad.

Plasma

Have you ever been exsanguinated,
drained tallow-gray, sapped, blanched,
neck tattooed with a vampire's snake eyes?

You can't remember how you got here,
who came at you in the dark.

That was then.

You lie in the tuneless sunlight,
wish you were an early riser,
a jogger, a follower of recipes.

The cat wants to be fed,
the day waits to be seized,
but all you can hold in your head
is last night's salty drool, TV remote,
boxed voices, the memory of plasma.

But there's no more blood to give.
He didn't leave you a platelet.

And still you rise,
pull your hair
into a bun.

Half-Life

Even dead, the flowers on the table are more beautiful
than anything else in this room – which is a fucking mess.
The kitchen sink's full of dirty dishes. I've run out of spoons.
The coffee cups have a thick brown silt cleaved to their wells.
It would take days of soaking to get them clean again.
Easier to throw them away.
Turns out ceramics, too, have a half-life.

A dry rose petal, sugared pink, lies on the table.
I flick it with my finger, watching it rise
into the dust-mote air, take flight for two seconds,
hovering, before I snatch it, crush it in my palm,
breathe in its sweet oily scent, hoping
to cover over the stench of ammoniacal piss
rising from the cat box like an unholy incense.

A metallic-green bottle fly buzzes against the windowpane,
determined, looking for escape, for air,
the purifying blue of sky.
I must find a way to do the same – find a way to breathe again.
Dig myself out of the sink.

Try

a cube
of ice
in a tall glass of milk.
Try
a mayonnaise and red onion
sandwich.
Try
the cold
pickled pigs' feet.
Try
swimming out through bladderwort
& reeds, ankles tangled.
Try
to untangle
yourself.
Try
to live
without holding your breath.

The Earth Is Flat

The earth is flat. I know this for a fact.
I've seen swans disappear over the blue horizon
in a quick-time blink, like ducks going over Niagara.
I've seen sharks that breach the open sky,
snapping at gulls in flight, then tumble off-screen
with feathers in their jaws.
The world is flat, the world is flat.
Like too-much-Prozac flat. Like not-enough-Prozac flat.
Like a-holy-grail-that-can-never-be-found flat.
Like earthenware-brown.

You claim the earth is round.
Perhaps it was, once, long ago.
And, true, when you're near me –
when the kitchen becomes evil,
and the world opens its legs like she did for *you*,
then I cannot say the earth is flat.
Then the earth becomes a sieve,
a colander of salad greens I drip through like plasma.
You mop me up, rinse me off in the sink,
watch me circle the drain. And think that's love.

But you're wrong: I was peeling onions,
that's why I cried – not for you,
but for potato peels and sour milk.

I am not you. I see things as truth,
believe in nothing but flat earth and pancakes
that will not bubble or rise.
She calls me, you know – every morning
as I scramble for momentum –
to remind me you are gone.
Grief overtakes the spooning of soil onto my plate.

Because I know the earth is flat.
I've seen it. I've foraged for greens in the sea,
seen white-tailed deer running across
the ocean floor, galloping away from me,
as *you* did. And elephant dung,
masses of it washing up onshore.
They're down there too – giant pachyderms
holding their ground at the horizon line,
searching out conch shells and sea cucumbers,
their massive trunks swaying with the current,
slow dancing in kelp forests, near where the deep waters
spill over into darkness and empty sky,
leaving nothing but a trail of murky italics.
Words with no meaning. *I hate you.*

And my children cry blood tears for me,
watch me in the dwindling distance
swallowing swans, choking on the pin-sharp beaks of their young,
watch as I teeter on the knife-edge of the world,
hanging on to the last outcropping branch,
listing toward a nothingness that can't be countered.

That simply *is*. That is a fact.
Like flat earth. Like scorched earth.
My life in five words: Burned. To. The. Ground.
Cindered.

Will I rise from the ashes or stay here clinging,
legs dangling, praying for the swans in my belly –
hoping they, at least, will survive my fall.
Or that the elephants will wash me clean
in sea spray, tusk my shirt, pull me back up.
To reality. Or hope. Something tangible and pure.
Say, "Here's the deal: you vomit back up our goslings
and give us fresh-cut bales of hay,
and we'll show you the way back."
Okay, I say, okay.
And they say this: "If you can only remember that
the earth is *round* you will survive the fall. So let go."
Okay, I say, okay.

For Dorianne Laux – "Facts About the Moon"

I once heard you say it was Philip Levine who
taught you that poetry is raw precision –
taught you to aim true: to find the crosshairs
of every ant, acorn, honeycomb, leech.

Or maybe you always knew how to throw a spear
straight into the heart of night,
pierce the moon, wrench it from the sky –
steal the moon to make us miss it.

You taught me that poetry could wake me –
that I could cry for trees, for mad men,
for your lunar mother. For mine.
I am profoundly sad that I can never read your words again
for the first time.

Shrink Wrap

1.

"Help me," I said when I lay on the leather couch
for the first time.
The throw pillows were in my mother's colors – maroon and pine.
I hated them from the corners of my eyes.
I could hear his grizzled pause as he sucked on a cough drop,
cleared his ancient phlegmy throat.v

"Tell me change is possible. Tell me you can fix me."
I stared at the skylights in his sharp-pitched ceiling,
three rectangles of clean, uninterrupted blue,
and worried the sky could read my lips.

"I'll do my best," he said.
And I thought: That's not good enough.
Tell me you can do what I cannot. Lie to me.

2.

In the yard behind his office
a Chinese elm grew into the sky.
Once, he told me, there were two trees,
but one had withered and died
when his neighbors re-landscaped.

He told me about taproots —
that every tree has one single root it cannot live without.
They had severed it by mistake.

"Who is your taproot?" he asked.
And I cried in his office for the first time.

3.

But always: Tomorrow I'll be better. Tomorrow I will start.
I will start someday, until all the somedays are over.

4.

"Maybe I need to accept my limitations.
Maybe I should stop trying to break through the rock
and accept that I need to go around it."
But Dr. G said: "The Fat Lady hasn't sung yet."
"What will she sing when she does?"
"*Why* am I in this battle? *What's* behind the rock?"
I felt my mind grasping at his straws.
Outside, the gardeners were mowing.
I could barely hear him.

5.

"I cannot – I *cannot* – turn fifty still feeling like a pathetic child.
It's unbearable," I said. "It's absurd."
"But you *are* a child. You will always be a child –
you were born a child and you will die a child.
Who else can you be besides your mother's child?"

6.

I'm afraid the doctor has to cancel your appointment today –
he's in the hospital.
Will he be all right?
Unfortunately, he's closing his practice effective immediately.
*Can he speak on the phone? Will I have a chance
to say goodbye to him?*
He feels it would be unfair. Better to say goodbye once.
But we never said goodbye . . .
That's the only kind of closure he can give you now.

7.

I will start someday, until all the somedays are over.

8.

Six years, four times a week. My rattle-cough shrink.
My father, my mentor, keeper of wisdom, keeper of secrets,
sitting behind me, his walker beside him,
his bright spiffy tie, colorful socks – a protest against age.
Sweet and tough, witty and ancient, saving me every day.

I picture him on his deathbed, a small boy, a tiny child
crying out at the last moment of life for his mother.

9.

I look out at the sunrise sky, try to feel,
try to remember, commit his lessons to memory.
What am I supposed to do? What was it he said?
But I can't remember a single fucking thing. I can't.
I can't go on without your road map.
And he says, through the pink wind and clouds:
There is no road.

10.

I wrote him a love letter this afternoon –
a letter he will never read. And I said, at the end,
"Unfortunately, Dr. G, very unfortunately, we have to stop now."
Because that is what he would have said.
That is what he meant by goodbye.

SIX

Have Faith

I'm thinking about when I thought I knew.
I'm thinking about when the dog gets up
to stretch his legs – the way his whole body yawns.
I'm thinking about his soft coat. His blind love.
His blessing in this silent house.

My rings are made of amber, rubies, diamonds.
Each jewel an apology. "I'll be better.
We'll grow old together. Sit in rocking chairs," he said.
"Have faith."
Stay. Stay again. Again. Again.

I'm thinking about the Pope,
who stands on his balcony blessing us,
making promises even to those of us
who do not believe in things
beyond water and earth.

At the top of the stairs, my dog appears,
his warm fishy pant sensing sadness.
Just now, he was standing by the front door,
watching the street, vigilant,
protecting me better than any false prophet.

I think about my sons, my rangy boys already bitter
with irony and disbelief, who carry their secrets too close –
secrets I want to know so I can carry them to safety,
past the shoals and rapids and hidden rocks.
Promise them only good things wait.

I think about the future, the unknown,
unknowing – the Pope, who *claims* to know.
And is it better to face the truth,
or to buy the sow's-ear purse
that takes away despair?

I think about the river running, its sweet fresh water
born every moment, again and again,
rushing blindly toward a future it cannot see.
And wonder: Would the river stop,
refuse to spring forth from the earth's womb,

if it knew that stone by stone, bend by bend,
town by town, it leaves behind forever
the green hills, the speckled trout, the cresses?
That the sea it races to meet lies in wait
to swallow it? Salt it?

That soon its fresh waters will carry
swimmers to their deaths, sharks to their prey,
corpses to the depths, the dark final cold.
That sweet pure river. Would it stop if it knew?

For Jimmy

The day I prayed for Jimmy,
I walked along the stretch of beach,
beyond umbrellas and volleyball games.
It was already hot at 8 a.m.
Mid-tide, and the ocean was ideal.

Occasionally, pebbles skittered avalanche-y
down the cliff-like sand dunes.
I hurried past, just in case. I think of the second tower.
The beach was empty here.
Just one creepy naked man in the distance
lying sunward, tanning his penis.

I sat on the damp at the water's edge and closed my eyes,
prayed for Jimmy. Please, God. Prayed for my beautiful crazy kiwi.
Scruffy-headed piratical fool. Foolhardy, fearless.
Who'd wept in my arms that night, body shaking with fear,
cancer eating away at his spine.
I held him, lied to him. *I promise I won't let you die.*

Please. Give me a sign, proof that you exist.
I apologize for my doubts – but that's just how you made me.
But give me a sign and I promise I'll believe.
I opened my eyes and, in that instant,
a massive fin rose from the waves, black and jagged,

right there, in the shallows: a great white
splicing the surface of the sea.

I followed it along the shoreline,
watching it disappear and reappear.
Under the water it was invisible.
I could easily have gone in for a quick dip five feet from it
and never sensed it coming for me until I felt the sandpaper shove.
Cancer is like that.

The naked man got up, stretched,
strutted toward the water for a swim.
I shouted at him to stop,
pointing to the danger only I could see.
He shook his head. *I can't hear you.* Kept walking, smug,
penis and balls thwacking his thigh.

I pointed to the sea, the black fin now visible,
shearing the air.
He saw.
He stopped.

I promise I won't let you die.

Wisteria

I agree with you that wisteria
is beautiful when it blooms,
its lacy bowers dripping
with pale southern gentility.
But in winter, when it has dropped
its poisoned pea pods, its arsenical beans
tempting my dogs into a suicide pact,
wisteria bares its bones.
Skeletal twists of vines festoon the roofline,
a dusty macramé of dead twigs,
rats' nests hidden in its slings,
revealing telephone wires
against a blank blue sky,
reminding me of my mortality.
Until spring arrives, and once again
a flush of grape-like blooms
come back to hide the truth
for another season.

Cambridge Scientists Reverse Aging Process in Rat Brain Stem

They're close to finding a cure for death, but I will miss it.
Turns out aging is just another disease –
like diabetes or the Plague.
Which means, from the moment we're born,
every day we live is the disease progressing.

I reject death. I want to stop it in its tracks.
It's the one thing Walt Disney and I
have in common: part of me occasionally
thinks about being frozen alive.

And yet that bright blue jug I found
at the estate sale – a dead woman's jug –
outlived her and will outlive *me*.
I think about smashing it, burying it,
but what's the point?
Eventually it will be unearthed,
glued back together,
and land in the British Museum.

And What of the Afterlife?

1.

Far from Ajax,
a plum sits
on a
rocky shore,
sunburnt and
pruning.
The godhead
contemplates
its legless misery
and feels no pity.

2.

In the shallow basin of the
black lotus bowl beside my bed
a solid ash of incense
holds its fecal shape.
I burned it this morning,
praying for answers from the gods.

All I have found is this:
a pellet of hope,

ashes in a cracked clay bowl
on an oak table,
next to a plastic bottle of
flat Diet Coke and
a half-eaten pear.
Perhaps these are the only
answers they have.

3.

Black cat, ladder.
God or Tarot.
A wizened, kerchiefed gypsy
in a cheap storefront.
A minister in a white collar
preaching from the pulpit.
Do you believe in magic?
Life would be so much better
with an afterlife.

4.

Out on the lake a swan
becomes peckish, jittery,
and begins to clean herself,
sneaking occasional smells of her
underarms. Do not judge her.

Do you think a pigeon smells any better?
Or a gannet?
We cannot help who we are born to be.
Pasta noodle, fig or quince.
At some point we are all
reborn as beetles.

The Days Ahead

I pluck an errant hair from between my breasts.
These days the wild hairs pop up everywhere –
nipple, chin, stomach, thigh, bikini line.
I can't keep up with myself, stay groomed
and nit-picked. I need a mother gorilla.
These days my age begins to show
and the days, these days, too often filled
with the wild hair of gloom.

We're meant to regret the past, but I regret the future.
I regret the things I have not yet lost,
I regret the things I will never know.
I'll never learn to play the oboe, speak Chinese,
buy a blue-shuttered house in Greece.
Or, after all these years, finally learn
the correct way to fill an ice tray.
Have I ever been truly loved,
the way you read about in books?
Now only barren womb and forward movement,
the road behind me dwindling to a ribbon of blue
in the desert, a heaty, oil-slick haze,
taking daily steps forward into the oxygen of regret.

Yet still, some days, these days, when I trace the lifelines
on my palms, the spider veins and webs of ancient

stretch marks still faintly visible from giving birth
to someone else's future, I allow myself to hope,
for all of us, that ahead lies an evergreen forest
with a blanket of snow, bright red berries on a silvery branch
and deepening hues.

A Peacock's Beauty

I.

I wake too tired to make the rounds again, the endless spin.
Lately, when I get out of bed, before it has time
to reset itself, my face looks like it's dripping,
an ancient glass window, water sheeting down itself.
A bead of sweat slips from under my breast,
finds a trickling path, lands, triumphant, inside my belly button.

Dog-time, and the peacock's tail seems too blue-green to bear.
He struts so proudly across the garden,
sorry for us that we can never be as beautiful.
Oh, for a single feather, a bright blaze of his beauty
in this gray swamp, a last remaining tendril of gold.
What once was fresh, strong and clarion,
now nothing more than liquid sand, melting
year by year, decade by decade, century by century.
Quatrefoils of colored glass moving toward their doom.

I drive to my mother's house at dusk,
past the wide glassy bay, two swans gliding,
perfect pink intònico blush on the water,
the mirrored sky. Stupidly perfect. Painfully beautiful.
And all I can think is: Fuck this. I love it all so much
and someday I'm going to die – never again

see the drooping peonies, my children, tiny green leaves
coming back to life on a spring linden.
Never taste a lemon rind.
"I forgot the peanuts," I say,
and kiss my mother's papery cheek.
"There's ice in the bar. I'm drinking a martini.
Did you see that sky? The swans are back."

2.

I stretch my arms to the dimming sky,
let the sweat from my breasts, my underarms,
my anger and lust evaporate into the ether.
I want my DNA to find eternity.
If I seal a drop of my sweat, a flake of dry skin,
in a glass vial, will I still exist a thousand years
from now? A fly in amber? Does amber drip?
The slow drip, drip – my morning face, my morning
sweat, mourning for immortality, for the end before it comes.
I mourn for my children, even as I bring them into the world.
I mourn, I rail, at the unfairness of a peacock's beauty.

The Art of Falling

It rained a heavy rain last night,
a forceful punch-drunk deluge
that pummeled the ground with its fists.
Water overflowed the drainpipes,
splattered the leaves of the sycamore,
the line of flowering pears that never fruit.

But that's not what I was listening for
when I opened all the windows.
Not the *landing* – but the hissing, fulsome
sound of rain passing through a dark sky,
still journeying toward its destination.
It's the sound of rain *still* rain, not yet a puddle,
or an overfilled pool, or saturated earth,
that soothes me in my bed.

Water suspended, water falling.

I remember thinking that the jumpers from the second tower
looked like angels before they reached the ground.

Or is it the memory of summer days
running barefoot through a playground fountain
that the sound of falling rains instils in me?
Umbrellas of water, rainbows refracted in air,

as we danced in circles around the copper drains,
clothes soaked through and through,
and the pigeons watched, heads cocked,
waiting to slake their thirst once the antic children
began to shiver under the sun.

Water suspended, water falling

lulls me into a dreamless sleep, suspending me in time.
And I can forget
that I'm older than I want to be.
And I can forget
that I, too, will be absorbed by earth.
And I can forget that I am only passing through.

The Miracle of Chickens

Five fresh eggs in a basket were left on my doorstep
by the next-door neighbor. An apology for his
clueless rooster, who believes the dawn arrives at 3 a.m.

There are days when I lie in bed dreaming of the guillotine.
But then I think of his plump sister wives
– the miracle of chickens.
How they pee, shit, birth, spit out perfect hard-shelled eggs
all through the same tiny hole.

I take the eggs into the kitchen.
Crack them on the edge of a bowl.
Watch their pure yellow yolks
float to the top like sunrises.

What the Deep Water Knows

There is no alchemy in nature –
no turning wine to blood or tin to gold.
And yet, when I breathe in the warm fishy
smell of Horseleech Pond in late July,
stand knee-deep in its glass-clear waters
watching the blue heron stalk out from the secrets of the rushes,
my heart becomes a different heart, a quieter heart,
slowing to the circadian rhythms of the lilies.

There is no alchemy in nature but its own alchemy:
turning birds into horses, a hot, humid world to ice –
then back again when at last the sun forgave the earth –
turned the seas into a thoroughfare, scattering the cold world
onto distant shores. Glacial arks to transmute soil and sea
into pine forests. Melt into sweet-water ponds,
and the unseen springs that well inside me
when I wade out beyond the lily pads.

There is no alchemy in nature but its own alchemy.
No philosopher's stone. Only the drift and till,
the pebbles and rocks, borne here in the bellies of icebergs,
that pock the sandy shallows beneath my feet;
and the jagged stones along the shoreline
where box turtles take the sun.

There is no magic but this pond, these deep waters
I have swum in every summer of my life.
Water a million years old. Water that holds the tales
of sabretooths, and how the earth went dark.

Water that has held my body a thousand times,
knows the shape of my curves, the weight of my breasts,
how long I can hold my breath.
Water that can turn my heart from dun-gray lead to gold.
Where every swim loosens and smooths the ancient wounds,
the heaviness of millstones.
Water that when, one day, it changes shape again,
will carry my stories with it.